I0814520

Eric Liddell

Are you ready?

The true story of Eric Liddell and the Olympic Games

Catherine Mackenzie
Illustrated by Rita Ammassari

From the edge of the track a voice yelled, ‘On your marks, get set, GO!’

Eight excited schoolboys raced down the track. Eric was soon in front, his head back and his legs pumping. He broke through the finishing tape well ahead of the others.

He was one of the best athletes at Eltham College. Athletics was great fun. But it was hard being at boarding school, so far away from his parents in China. Eric longed to go back. Maybe he would one day. China was his home, even though he was British.

He broke through the finishing tape well ahead of the others.

When he got to his senior year, people started to talk about his future. 'Do you think Eric will be ready to run in the Olympics?' a teacher asked. 'He is, after all, the fastest man in Scotland.'

However Eric was getting ready for something else. Eric was going to speak to a crowd of people about Jesus Christ. 'I might not be ready to speak,' Eric thought to himself, 'but I know that God is ready to forgive those who trust in his Son, Jesus.'

That was what Eric had to tell his audience. 'I'm ready now,' he smiled.

Eric was going to speak to a crowd of people about Jesus Christ.

'Are you ready for church?' Eric's mother asked one Sunday morning. Eric wasn't a child anymore, he was a man, but it was still great to have his parents back in Scotland.

During the holidays, all the Liddells, including Eric's brothers, Robert and Ernest, and his sister, Jennie, stayed together in Edinburgh. Sunday was a special day for the Liddell family – it was a day set aside for God. They gathered with other people who loved Jesus, listened to the Bible and sang praises to God the Father.

Sunday was a special day for the Liddell family.

'Eric's in the Olympic team,' Jennie squealed. 'Isn't that wonderful? I'm sure he'll win!'

'I've got to get ready first,' Eric laughed. 'I've a lot of training to do.'

Eric had won lots of races over the years, at school and at university. However, he still had to keep fit in order to run his best. During one race, Eric showed how fit he really was.

'Eric's in the
Olympic team,'
Jennie squealed.

He had been tripped up accidentally by one of the other athletes. Everyone was sure that Eric had lost. However, he picked himself up and began to run again.

Yard after yard, Eric ran like the wind. Then he threw his head back, and the spectators knew something special was going to happen.

He caught up with the other runners, then he passed them and then he cut through the finishing tape. What a race! Eric was exhausted.

People were sure that Eric was ready for the Olympics now. He might even win a gold medal they thought.

Everyone was sure
that Eric had lost.

But later on, Eric heard that some of the Olympic events were being held on a Sunday.

Eric exclaimed, 'I won't run on the Lord's day! I am going to keep God's day holy.'

The British team did not want to lose Eric from the Olympic Games. There was only one thing for it. He would have to run in a completely different race – one he hadn't trained for. The 400 metres was a lot longer and harder than the 100-metre sprint he had been preparing for. Would Eric be ready in time?

Eric exclaimed, 'I won't run on the Lord's day!'

In the year 1924, the Olympics were taking place in Paris. The city was full of excited people waiting to watch the games.

When the 11th of July arrived, Eric was getting ready in the changing rooms. A piece of paper was put into his hand. There was a Bible verse on it that said, 'He who honours me I will honour.' This was really encouraging. The note reminded Eric that God was in charge of everything. Obeying God's Word was the best thing Eric could do.

The note reminded Eric that God was in
charge of everything.

As soon as the starter's pistol sounded, Eric was off down the track at full pelt. There was such a long way to go to the finishing tape. The spectators wondered if Eric would be able to keep up the pace.

One by one, Eric passed all the other athletes until he was up in front. Then he threw his head back and pumped his legs with all the energy he had. Eric Liddell was the winner. He thanked God for giving him the strength.

Eric Liddell was the winner. He thanked God for giving him the strength.

Once all the excitement was over, Eric left for China. He was ready for a new stage in his life. He was going to be a missionary like his parents.

Eric still competed in athletics now and again, but he spent most of his time telling others about Jesus. He also became a husband and father. Life was quite different now.

Once all the excitement was over, Eric left for China.

Life was different for lots of people. The Second World War had started. Europe and America were fighting Germany and Japan.

Eric put his wife and children on a boat for Canada, where they would be safe. They all hoped that he would join them soon. However, this did not happen. Nobody was ready for the Japanese when they attacked. Eric and others were put in a prisoner-of-war camp. They were badly treated by the soldiers, and many people suffered from disease.

Eric put his wife and children on a boat for Canada.

Eric tried to keep everyone's spirits up by organising games and races. Eric also told the prisoners about his loving Saviour, Jesus Christ.

Many in the camp were thankful for Eric's bright smile during those dark times. However, on the 21st of February 1945, Eric Liddell died in hospital.

The Bible says that Jesus has defeated death. Those who trust in him will receive forgiveness of sins and everlasting life. That was Eric's reward – far greater than an Olympic medal.

Eric also told the prisoners about his loving Saviour, Jesus Christ.

This book is written for Molly, Ailsa and Lowri.

May grace and peace be multiplied to you in the knowledge of God and of Jesus our Lord (2 Peter 1:2 ESV).

ISBN: 978-1-84550-790-9
Reprinted in 2016, 2022, 2023 and 2026

Published by Christian Focus Publications,
Geanies House, Fearn, Tain, Ross-shire, IV20 1TW,
Scotland, U.K.
www.christianfocus.com

Cover design by Daniel van Straaten
Printed by Imprint, India